2019 A-GEM (MEGA) Year

5779 The Year of Light & 2nd Chances

DR. CAROLYN G. ANDERSON

2019 A Gem Year

Book #3 of **The MEGALiFE Series**

Copyright © 2019 by Riley Press

All rights reserved. No part of this book may be reproduced or transmitted in any form or by any means, electronically or mechanically, including photocopying, recording, retrieval system, without prior written permission from the author, except for the inclusions of brief quotes in a review.

Published by Riley Press, a division of Integrity Consulting Enterprise, LLC

Book Cover and Interior designed by Riley Press

Printed in the United States of America. All scripture quotations, unless otherwise indicated, are taken from the Holy Bible, New International Version®, NIV®. Copyright ©1973, 1978, 1984, 2011 by Biblica, Inc.TM Used by permission of Zondervan. All rights reserved worldwide. www.zondervan.com The "NIV" and "New International Version" are trademarks registered in the United States Patent and Trademark Office by Biblica, Inc.TM

Other scripture references are noted and were either taken from the MSG, KJV, NKJV or AMP versions of the Bible. Non-scripture references are also noted within the text and will not have its own reference page.

Table of Contents

Dedication 9
   Prophetic Testimonials......................... 11
   Background 13
Introduction – A-GEM Year 19
Purpose of the Book 25
Preface 31
Chapter 1 – Spin Cycle 37
   The Year 2016 39
Chapter 2 – The Year 2017 45
Chapter 3 - The Year 5777....................... 51
Chapter 4 – New Leadership.................... 57
   Legal Authority 57
   The Remnants 57
Chapter 5 – Who Am I?............................ 65
Chapter 6 – Promises 71
Chapter 7 – Rosh Hashanah 77
   Head of the Year.................................. 77
   The Lord's Appointed Times 83
     Times and Seasons 85
     Numbers & Biblical Numerology .. 91
Chapter 8 –The Year 5779 97

Ayin Tet (pronounced like Tate) 97
The Year of 2nd Chances 101
Chapter 9 –Happy New Year 105
Chapter 10 –A-Gem (MEGA) Year 2019 111
Making Everyday Good Again 111
Light vs. Darkness 124
Infinity 127
Chapter 11 - Palace Time 129
Wealth Transfer 132
Chapter 12 – The Awakening 139
Summary 153
Confession 166
78 Decrees & Declarations 169
Personal Prayer 177
Appreciation 187
About the Author 189
Connect with us! 193
Other Books by Dr. Carolyn 195

Dedication

This book is dedicated to you as you

Make Everyday Good Again (MEGA)!

Prophetic Testimonials

When God's people need to hear a NOW word of the Lord, God sends Dr. Carolyn G. Anderson to let them know what He is saying for that season and time.

In 2017 The MVP Year, Dr. Carolyn brings forth the timing of the Lord when God will initiate 'the seven years of abundance as it was in the days of Joseph.

Dr. Carolyn is a Prophet who is compassionate, loving and anointed in this hour to bring forth the ministry of Royalty, Wealth and Health. This book is a must for those who have an ear to hear and an eye to see what the Spirit of the Lord is saying NOW!

Apostle K. Anthony
Kingdom Cathedral International Ministries

I established some grand goals for the beginning of 2016, so I was excited to petition heaven for manifestation. During the midpoint of 2016, I felt stuck. I decided to multi task by praying and doing my required work. I told God that I needed to hear a word from Him because I felt stuck.

When I got off work, I received a call from Prophet Carolyn telling me that she had a word for me. She shared a word that equipped and empowered me to move from feeling unstuck to ready to possess the land that God promised me. She is an on-time Prophet.

Latreeta Burns
Jericho Church Without Walls

Background

HAPPY 2019

The Prophetic calling on Dr. Carolyn's life can be traced back to her childhood. She was very discerning and oftentimes would know something was going to happen before it did. She would choose her friends wisely because God revealed the intentions of their hearts towards her and therefore she knew the right friends to hang around.

Subsequently, she made very wise choices because she could envision the results. There are very specific moments where Dr. Carolyn recalls making decrees (back then she just spoke not realizing what she was doing), about things to come in her life. There's one very specific moment in high school, where she told one of her best friends that Kevel (husband now) would be her husband within 10 years. She wasn't interested in him at that time not even as a boyfriend. It would so happen that ten years later, Kevel became her husband and still is to this day. There are numerous accounts where she would know specific dates and times of events including the birthdates of her children, prior to the occasion.

The prophetic calling on her life truly gave birth on 3.1.03, where she had an encounter with God and He blessed her with the gift of speaking in tongues and the prophetic anointing. It was from that moment that she would begin to flourish and realize that God speaks to her in various ways, especially through the alpha-numeric language, nature, and blessed her with the gift to understand times and seasons. She also has the gift of understanding the steps to wealth, healing and being very strategic.

To thresh the gift, she and her husband were both ordained as Apostles and Prophets and lead a Global Ministry that's transforming lives.

Most recently, God has given Dr. Carolyn very specific dates and times for the body so that they can understand His plans and purposes for their lives. Allow the messages within this text to speak to you and hopefully you will participate in God's timing and seasons.

The **TIME IS NOW!** It is the appointed time to begin your new journey and experience the FRESH START. Therefore, meet the **Fresh Voice** that God is using for such a time as this.

"There is a time for everything, and a season for every activity under the heavens:"
Ecc 3:1 NIV

 **Pause Moment……….**

Take a few minutes and just begin to write what you are hearing in your spirit. What are your desires? What are your 2019 Goals? What are some missed 2018 Goals, that you must accomplish in 2019? Just take this moment to pause, reflect on your life and write.

_____

_____

_____

_____

_____

_____

_____

_____

_____

Introduction – A-GEM Year

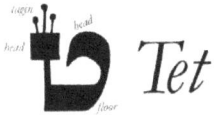

Welcome to the (**MEGA**) **A-Gem** Year, where God is **M**aking **E**verything **G**ood **A**gain as it was in the beginning. According to **Genesis 1:4,** it states that *"God saw that the light was good..."* Everything that God made in the beginning was good and as we embrace this good year, get ready to experience some new beginnings, as He's making all things **new** and **good** again. However, it requires your participation and intentionality. There is some work that needs to be done on your part.

 *"...And God saw that it was good:"*
Gen 1:18 NIV

For the past 16 years, I have been seeking God prior to the beginning of each new year for a theme or scripture for my immediate family for that year! He's given a word each time for the year. That word would carry us consistently throughout the year and it would become the bedrock on which we stand. What I mean by that is, whenever something arose that seemed contrary to the word that the Lord had given us, we would declare what God said about that particular year. This is how we were able to fight and combat what was happening in our lives. It also allowed us to live in peace and harmony throughout the year, because we knew that no matter what happened, it would turn out for our good, because God had given us a word for the year.

When my husband and I started Pastoring in 2011, we sought the Lord even further for a theme for the ministry. In addition to the general word for the church, each member received personal prophetic ministry. Consequently, we also started learning more about our Jewish roots and about God's biblical calendar, which is different from the Gregorian/Julius calendar that the western world is more familiar with. Nevertheless, with the new knowledge of God's biblical calendar, we lived according to both calendars, except our celebrations, observations, feasts and times of fasting are according to the Hebraic calendar.

During very specific appointed times with God, He revealed to me that He elevated me from being just a Prophet that minister's personal prophecies, to a Prophet on a Global basis that understands His timing and seasons and was a strategic voice that transform lives. From then leading up to today, I have been declaring the meaning of the YEARS and what God has in store for His people. Today, I don't have to seek God for the Word for the Year, because He has already given me the meanings for 49 years out, which means that you have everything you need to make everyday good again. Welcome to **<u>A-Gem Year</u>**, which is **MEGA** backwards, and this year already existed before the foundations of the World.

To fully participate in God's timing and seasons, one of the pre-requisites is to **Trust God!** Perhaps you had a rough 2018 and you're feeling like this year is just another year, and nothing special about it. However, what I am about to share with you about the uniqueness of 2019 and the Hebrew Year 5779 will change your perspective about the King. If you trust, believe and activate the steps in this book, I believe that you will live to tell about how good 2019 was and how God's Word is truth. Are you ready for the MEGA (A-Gem) **year**?

.

NOTES..........

Purpose of the Book

This book is the third of the MEGALiFE Series of books that runs on a seven (7) year cycle as it was in the days of Joseph the Dreamer and has been re-instituted by God. According to Genesis **41:25-30,32 NIV**

"Then Joseph said to Pharaoh, "The dreams of Pharaoh are one and the same. God has revealed to Pharaoh what he is about to do. [26] The seven good cows are seven years, and the seven good heads of grain are seven years; it is one and the same dream. [27] The seven lean, ugly cows that came up afterward are seven years, and so are the seven worthless heads of grain scorched by the east wind: They are seven years of famine. [28] "It is just as I said to Pharaoh: God has shown Pharaoh what he is about to do. [29] Seven years of great abundance are coming throughout the land of Egypt, [30] but seven years of famine will follow them. Then all the abundance in Egypt will be forgotten, and the famine will ravage the land. [32] The reason the dream was given to Pharaoh in two forms is that the matter has been firmly decided by God, and God will do it soon."

He is the same God then, today and forevermore, and chooses when He does what and with whom He chooses. Thus, God has re-established the seven (7) year cycle and I am the messengers that He is using, along with other Prophets to lead in this time and season and so join in on the Movement and move in God's timing.

The purpose of the book is to share what God is doing right **NOW** and what's to come and how you can participate in His timing so that **His will** be done on earth as it is in Heaven in your life. It's not by coincidence why you are reading this book. It is by divine appointment. God is Sovereign in all His ways, and you are a part of His Masterplan. I am so excited to share it with you and be on this wonderful journey in this MEGALiFE. You are about to experience some new and refreshing things and I believe that it will be a **good** year for you. According to Amos 3:7 NIV it says, ***"Surely the Sovereign Lord does nothing without revealing his plan to his servants the Prophets."*** Well, God has revealed some amazing things, so let the revelations flow to you as you read this book.

God has a set time for everything and He desires for His people to be in sync with His timing so that we can truly live out our purposes and kingdom mandates. Don't you want to hear "well done, my good and faithful servant?" I know I do. I have purposed in my heart that I will get to heaven empty, meaning that I would have used every gift He has given me, lived life fully and maximized my purpose to its fullest potential.

Life is easier and more peaceful when one understands God's timing. It makes you wiser and makes the journey of life more pleasant and harmonious.

According to Psalm 90:12 NIV, it says, ***"Teach us to number our days, that we may gain a heart of wisdom"*** and Job 14:5 NIV says *"A* *person's days are determined; you have decreed the number of his months and have set limits he cannot exceed."* Thus, knowing what season of life you are in and where you are going plays an intricate role in your destiny.

According to Ecclesiastes 3:1-8 NIV
"There is a time for everything, and a season for every activity under the heavens: a time to be born and a time to die, a time to plant and a time to uproot, a time to kill and a time to heal, a time to tear down and a time to build, a time to weep and a time to laugh, a time to mourn and a time to dance, a time to scatter stones and a time to gather them, a time to embrace and a time to refrain from embracing, a time to search and a time to give up, a time to keep and a time to throw away, a time to tear and a time to mend, a time to be silent and a time to speak, a time to love and a time to hate, a time for war and a time for peace."

Are you ready to live the **MEGALiFE**™? Are you ready for your fresh start and your new beginning? It's time to make millions, to live in excess, always having more than enough. It's time for the Abundance as it was in Genesis! So, get ready for the #**MEGALiFE**™ because it belongs to you.

NOTES..........

Preface

Before going forward and sharing the good things about the year **5779/2019**, let's first do a quick recap so that there's a better understanding and a more in-depth knowledge, as to why God is **Making Everyday Good Again** and the restarting the 7-year cycle.

The years **2015** and **2016** were years when God did a pause and shift some things and people around. He had to do this because there were some that were declaring that destruction was forthcoming. Yet, myself and a few other Prophets were not sensing that's what God was doing. God was sharing that there's a great abundance coming, and while there's a great abundance coming, it would include some tests.

Every great move of God requires a season of testing. It was so in biblical days and it's so today. I believe that it was this foreshadowing of the tests that were being perceived as destruction and judgement.

Prophets are able to foresee certain things and at times when it's not clear, they tend to lean more towards, God sending judgement. It's not a bad thing, as one of the appointed roles of a Prophet is to rebuke and correct. The Prophets of the old were used as messengers of God prior to His judgements as a warning for the people to repent and turn from his or her wicked ways. Prophets also edify and are messengers of love, hope and prosperity.

Therefore, since Prophets are to subject themselves one to another, I did just that. I laid low per se and just listened to what others were saying, until I had further clarification from God.

The enemy is very cunning, and I have come to know some of his tactics and it would NOT have been a good thing for Prophets to be arguing and debating against each other publicly. That would be chaotic and create confusion and doubt and that's exactly what the enemy wanted. Therefore, the wise thing to do at that time, is simply to wait on God for more clarification.

It turns out that God was doing a major shifting and transition, such as the changing of guards and handing the baton to a new set of leaders whom He had prepared to lead in this season. This is no different from Moses to Joshua, Elijah to Elisha, Paul to Timothy and so forth. Remember, He's the same God then, today and forevermore, and so what He did then, God is still doing today. He was passing the baton to the new leaders that were qualified to lead in this generation.

These leaders, such as I had gone through the tests, remained in deep communion with God to hear His new strategies and revelations. God is such a gentleman and very respectful and therefore He does not speak in the noise. He speaks only when you have the time to truly hear what He has to say and oftentimes that requires moments of extended consecration and alone time with God.

Therefore, the years **2015** and **2016** were years that were pause moments and testing. While there were many ups and downs, trials and tribulations and some victories, what God was doing was necessary to get us to where we are today and the years to come. They were preparation years for the Abundance as it was in the days of Joseph. Many had experienced the Pit, Potiphar's House and the Prison Seasons and were patiently awaiting the **Palace** Season. That moment is here now, so embrace it.

Moments of Reflection......................

Pause and take a moment and reflect back on previous years. Write down what you can remember about those years.

_____

_____

_____

_____

_____

_____

_____

_____

_____

_____

_____

Chapter 1 – Spin Cycle

Life is a journey and not a final destination and, on that journey, there are seasons and cycles that exists. The seasons are a compilation of different processes and sometimes one season can be longer than the other. One of my favorite character in the bible is Joseph the Dreamer. To me, he's the epiphany of what it means to go through seasons and cycles of life. One of the most fascinating moments that's described in the bible is that **before** Joseph entered one of his last seasons (the Palace), the bible said, he changed his clothes. *"So, Pharaoh sent for Joseph, and he was quickly brought from the dungeon. When he had shaved and changed his clothes, he came before Pharaoh." Genesis 41:14 NIV*

Why would God use a metaphor of changing **clothes** as an expression for Joseph leaving his prison season before entering the new palace season? God could have used anything, but he chose clothes. There are many explanations, such as, clothes being a covering and how at times, one needs to change his or her alignment and affiliation to enter a new season. In this case, God's expression of clothing represents one of the processes of a test before a promotion.

The changing of clothes is an analogy to understand times and seasons in its simplest form. It was the perfect example for describing the years 2016, leading up to 2017, 2018 and the 2nd chances in 2019. Allow me to continue with the historical perspective so that I can share the full meaning of the significance and importance of the **Year 2019 and 5779**. The year 2019 is a year of 2nd Chances, A- Gem (MEGA) Year and 5779 is Ayin Tet (good).

The Year 2016

The year **2016** was like a Spin Cycle that occurs during the process of doing laundry. It was a year that had many ups and downs, trials and tribulations, some victories, and a feeling that words couldn't describe. There were many Christians that lost hope, and some came to the verge of totally giving up. Perhaps you were one of them that felt like 2016 was a world-wind year. One minute when it seems like things were going great, suddenly it was disappointment and brokenness. Just when things seemed hopeful, it was deferred. Some people literally became physically ill, while waiting for a change.

Just like doing a load of laundry, there's a process that must take place to get to the finished product. There's a process to get the clothes clean and ready to wear again, which represents the changing of seasons. This process of getting dirty laundry to clean clothes cannot be accomplished with just one equipment. It requires two equipment's, a washer and a dryer. God is saying that to succeed in this next seven years of abundance that's at hand, it will require divine alignments, strategic collaborations, unity and togetherness to thrive and be victorious.

Like any process there are steps that are necessary to have a quality product or result. The laundry process is a four-step process. First the clothes are washed, rinsed, then the spin cycle, then dried. The spin cycle is the step before putting the clothes in the dryer. If the clothes are not **removed** after the spin cycle and placed in the dryer, they will begin to smell.

When doing laundry, there are different options to choose from for when washing and drying. Depending on the type and color of the garments, the cycle can either be hot, cold, warm or a combination of both. Not all cycles will be the same. The same is true for going through tests. They don't all look alike. For me personally, I knew that God was healing my emotional ups and downs and some traumatic situations that entered my life during the earlier stage of my marriage.

The spin cycle in **2016** was necessary as it was meant to squeeze out the last ounce of heaviness so that we could enter the new finishing cycle of 2017, start walking in the **MEGA** Year of 2018, and experience a 2nd Chance of the in 2019. God had to heal some wounds, some deep soul wounds, emotional and relational issues, brokenness, financial drought and some heavy burdens that His people were carrying. The clothes needed to be changed and those that were pressed needed to so that they met the prerequisite to enter the Palace Season. This was a set-up for NOW!

Moments of Reflection......................

Pause and take a moment and reflect back on the year **2016 and 2017.** Did you go through any tests or trials? Did you experience any healing during **2016**? Do you know what God had to squeeze out of you, if anything?

_____

_____

_____

_____

_____

_____

_____

_____

_____

_____

Chapter 2 – The Year 2017

Seventeen – the number of Victory

The year **2017** was the year of the **MVP** (Manifestations, Victo-ries (Re's), Purpose and Promises being established). It was the year for healing and being in good health and it was God's **RESET year.** It was a year of preparation for the **SEVEN YEAR CYCLE** as it was in the days of Joseph the dreamer, starting with the seven years of Abundance as written in Genesis 41:29 NIV *"Seven years of great abundance are coming..."*

The number seventeen (17) has been associated with VICTORY. Before I did the research on the number 17, God revealed to me that 2017 was the year of many **VICTO-RIES and the (Re's),** such as re-set, re-demption, re-velation, re-newal, re-stitution and so on. He said many victories will **MANIFEST** in 2017. Many had suffered in 2016 and so 2017 was the comeback year. Part of this GREAT VICTORY was the mass healing that took place in many people's life. I wrote about this healing in my #1 Best Selling Book, **Heal-thy LiFE - Heal-thy Land**, where I expressed that the first place that the word healing appears in the bible is Genesis 20 vs. 17. This wasn't a coincidence. God knew that before the foundations of the world that the year 2017 would start the healing process all over again. Many had not experienced healings in previous years for various reason, and God wanted His people to know that they don't need to look for a cure or accept bad news, because He sent His Good News to heal every disease and to set us free.

In the Bible the number 17 symbolizes "overcoming the enemy" and "complete victory." God overcame the sins of rebellious humans when he flood the earth through rain on the 17th of the second Hebrew month. Noah's ark and its eight passengers rested on the mountains of Ararat on the 17th of the seventh month (right in the middle of God's annual Holy time known as the Feast of Tabernacles).

Jesus Christ gained a complete victory over death and the grave when God resurrected him near sunset on Nisan 17 (Saturday, April 8, 30 A.D.) (This paragraph taken from biblestudy.org)

In the year 2017, God renewed His Covenant with you as He declared in Genesis 17:1-17. Whether you knew it or not, you are a part of the covenant of Abraham and his descendants. Whether you are a Jew or a Christian you are part of the covenant because you are one of Abraham's descendants. You are a part of God's Royal family. *"When Abram was ninety-nine years old, the Lord appeared to him and said, "I am God Almighty; walk before me faithfully and be blameless. Then I will make my covenant between me and you and will greatly increase your numbers." Abram fell facedown, and God said to him, "As for me, this is my covenant with you: You will be the father of many nations. No longer will you be called Abram; your name will be Abraham, for I have made you a father of many nations. I will make you very fruitful; I will make nations of you, and kings will come from you. I will establish my covenant as an everlasting covenant between me and you and your descendants after you for the generations to come, to be your God and the God of your descendants after you."*

Abraham didn't know how God was going to fulfill the promises. He didn't know the process. He just believed that if God spoke something then it's true. God has spoken that you have a victorious life and therefore it's up to you to believe it, own it and start taking the necessary steps toward your destiny. You have a **MEGA LiFE**™ at hand and it's your time.

Moments of Reflection......................

Take a moment and pause and reflect on the year 2017. Did you experience any victories or Re's? Perhaps relocation, re-marriage, renewal, reset, restitution, replevin? Any MVP's? Take a moment and write about your 2017.

_____

_____

_____

_____

_____

_____

_____

_____

_____

Chapter 3 - The Year 5777

Earlier in the Introduction, I shared about God's **Biblical calendar** and the Gregorian calendar, which is the one you're probably more familiar with. God established His biblical calendar so that the Children of Israel would remember Him and set aside certain times as appointed times with Him. While we are no longer operating under the law of Moses, God's biblical calendar still exists.

There are certain set times that are days to observance and are God's set times. One of those times is **Rosh Hashanah** (usually around September or October) and **Yom Kippur** also known as The Day of Atonement. Rosh Hashanah is considered the Head of the Year or the Civilian New Year. It is believed to be the time that God made civilization (Adam and Eve). Therefore, every year around this time, the Jewish people and other Kingdom followers will observe this day and the 10 days of awe (**Yom Kippur**) thereafter. Yom Kippur is God's Highest Holy Day out of all the appointed times. It is said to be the day that God forgives our sins and re-start our lives with His blessings.

Our immediate family celebrates Rosh Hashanah, Yom Kippur and the other appointed days to honor God and to show Him that we believe His Word and are participating with His times and seasons. We have seen tremendous blessings in our lives, since wholeheartedly following the Hebraic Calendar, including honoring the Sabbath Day as a holy day and a day of rest.

The year 5777 was the year of the **Triple Crown**, the year of God **perfecting some things in His people.** It was the year of completion, resets, and the year of **divine rest**. This is not a rest where you do nothing, but rather rest from the enemy and the celebration of Victories. If you follow God's calendar and the Gregorian calendar, you get to enjoy and celebrate three (3) New Year which are: (1) Rosh Hashanah, (2) January 1st and (3) Nisan (around March-April), which is the Biblical New Year- the time when the children of Israel had the Great Exodus from Egypt. The Jewish people celebrate this time also as a re-start of God's calendar. God loves celebrations and He loves to give opportunities to start over, just like every new day.

Therefore 5777/2017 was a great year in the lives of God's people and it was the perfect year for God to assign new leaders as a reset for the seven years of Abundance that's at hand. He is truly a great father and I hope that you are ready to experience the **MEGALiFE** Movement.

 **Moment...................**

What are your Aha thus far? What revelation/s did you receive, or did you learn anything new that you didn't know before?

_____

_____

_____

_____

_____

_____

_____

_____

_____

_____

_____

Chapter 4 – New Leadership

Legal Authority

The tests and trials you've had up to this point, were your pre-qualifications for the promotions in the Kingdom of God. In every era, whether it's the biblical days or today, at certain timeframes God will change guards and appoint new leaders to carry on the race. The baton has to be passed from one runner to the next, so that the team can win the race. If it's not passed, then the race does not continue.

The Remnants

God has raised up a generation that He's calling the **NOW GENERATION**. These are those in their 20's, 30's, 40's, 50's and some 60's and 70's that have not gotten their opportunity to lead and will now get that opportunity. He's raising up a new set of leaders and warriors to carry the baton as the race continues to the finish line. There's one particular generation that God is distinctly using as the Leaders for today and that's Generation X. Gen X are those born between 1965 to 1976 – and in 2019 are ages 43-54. Out of all the generations, they have the shortest range in years, with only 11 years. All other generations age ranges are between 18 to 21 years. For example, Gen Y, affectionately known as the Millennials, were born between 1977 to 1995 and today are ages 23-42 with a range of 18 years.

God revealed that Gen X have been x'ed out and passed over for years and now He is giving them the opportunity to lead. There are so many conferences and resources for Millennials and oftentimes no mention of any other age group. Typically, the Baby Boobers (born between 1946-1964) will mentor and train the Millennials but forget about Gen X. God said Gen-X have been the silent generation, the un-mentored, the cast outs and the forgotten, but He has not forgotten them. God will never allow His order to be out of place and so Generation X cannot be left out and passed over anymore and God himself says He has given the baton to them to lead and to train others.

As we embrace the #**MEGA (A-Gem)** Year, God is also doing some age reversals, renewals and resets and so the 43's will now feel and look like the 34-year-old and so on. There will be a change from the Moses' to the Joshua's. From the Elijah's to the Elisha's and from the Naomi's to the Ruth's. These new leaders are the Remnants. God is raising up a Joshua generation with the Key of David, with the Joseph's Anointing and the spirit of Deborah to fulfill all of God's prophetic promises to Israel and His Beloved Church. While God is releasing the **FRESH VOICES** (*the Joshua's, Joseph's, Ester's, Deborah's to birth forth something new;* He still need the Paul's, Elisha's, Peter's and so on, to be mentors and guides as they impart their wisdom and lead authentically.

Don't Hold on to the Baton

Sometimes those that have labored for years, can get envious when a new kid comes on the block per se. However, God is saying, oh I have not forgotten anyone. He's using the Elijah's to build up the Elisha's and the reward is GREAT. All will inherit and receive his or her reward.

You're Chosen

I believe that you are reading this book not by coincidence or accident, but by divine appointment. It doesn't matter what age group or generation you fall within, you are part of God's **MEGA YEAR** and **MEGA PLAN**. I believe that God wants you to know that it's time for you to truly walk in your authentic purpose and be a leader in your own sphere of influence. Do you know what you were called to be and to do? Are you crystal clear on your authentic purpose?

It's Your Time

You had to go through the pain, trials, tribulations and sufferings in the past, because pain precedes purpose. It wasn't until Joseph the Dreamer went through his moments of pain, that he truly gave birth to his purpose. You had to experience the contractions and the birthing pains. It was designed by God to give you authority and influence in certain areas of life. You can't have an anointing or authority in any area of life unless you've first walked through it. For you to be victorious in anything and to have legal authority you must first experience it, be tested in it, so that you can have dominion over it.

To have wealth you must first know what it's like to be broke. To have authority in healing you must first be healed, which means that you had to be sick in some area of your life (financial, health, business etc.,) so that you have the anointing in that area to help others overcome. Jesus had to go through the test and trials and even death to win. He experienced temptation from the enemy. He experienced persecution. He paid the price and it was after the test, the spin cycle, that God granted Him the reward and gave Him the church as His bride. It was all a part of God's divine plan. So, it is for you.

Look at your life, the problems and heartaches are not in vain. It was God's way of granting you legal permission and authority over that area and now you can help someone else and build up the Kingdom of God. You've probably been broken enough for two or three people and are ready for the change. Your patience was a blessing so congratulations. It's time to walk in your **#MEGA YEAR**. According to James 1:12

AMP, it says *"Blessed (happy, to be envied) is the man who is patient under trial and stands up under temptation, for when he has stood the test and been approved, he will receive the victor's crown of life which God has promised to those who love Him."* Get your clothes ready, it's time to step into your royal season and wear that golden crown.

Moments of Reflection..................

Do you believe that you were called to lead?

_____

_____

_____

_____

Chapter 5 – Who Am I?

"The greatest tragedy in life is not death, but it's life without meaning, without a purpose"

Dr. Myles Munroe

The Year 2018 was truly the year to start establishing one's purpose. If you missed solidifying your authentic purpose in 2018, you have been given a second chance in 2019. Are you excited that we serve a God of 2nd Chances? In order to live the **MEGALiFE**™ and enjoy the fullness of God's timing, it's imperative to know the reason why God created you, because it will help you to know what you should be doing at this time. This is not the time to be a replicable of someone else or a carbon copy of another person's life. This is your time and your season. You've probably heard this before and it's very likely that because your life has been so difficult that you don't believe it's your time or your season to shine. It is possible, though, that you may have hoped and believed that it was your time, but you weren't truly living, breathing and being the authentic you. Oftentimes, this is what I have observed in my Clients, Coachee's and Students that I train and teach about Purpose. They sought their purpose in unbelief, until they take my Purposefinder coaching.

This season, living in the **MEGA** Year requires intentionality and being purposeful on living the good life. The late Dr. Myles Munroe said, ***"The greatest tragedy in life is not death, but life without meaning, without a purpose."*** Therefore, it's time to truly live life with meaning, so that you know where you fit in and which of the 10 spheres of influence you should dominion in. This is also referred to as the seven (7) mountains and I have added three (3) more areas to the existing seven. What area/s of influence do you believe that you are called to? Are you called to have influence and dominion in Business, Media, Family, Arts & Entertainment, Ministry, Government and/or Education? Perhaps it's in **Healthcare, Finance** or **Science & Technology? (The three God gave me to add).**

Sometimes you are called to more than one area and you may even find yourself being able to navigate in all the areas but knowing at least which sphere of influence (mountain) is your primary one will make life easier and more peaceful. Oftentimes when one is not sure of who he or she was born to be and do, confusion is eminent.

Dr. Myles Munroe (1992) also said **"fulfillment in life is dependent on becoming and doing what one was born to be and do. Anything less makes life an enemy and death a friend**." It is essential, vital, crucial and necessary that there's understanding of the fundamental principle of purpose and pursue it wholeheartedly. For without purpose, life has no direction and those who don't know where they are going will probably end up somewhere else. It's my desire and more importantly, God's desire that you live the **#MEGALiFE™** because everyday can be good again if you want it.

You are alive for such a time as this, so activate your PURPOSE and walk it out. Ask God what is your purpose in life? He will answer you. If you need guidance to get started on understanding your purpose, you can find resources on my website at www.carolynganderson.com. Start decreeing that you are living your season of the **MEGALiFE™** and don't stop decreeing it, until you feel and see it.

Now it's time for a Pause Moment. Take some time and jot down what you believe your Purpose in life is. If you know your Purpose Statement or Vision Statement, write it down as well. Finally write down which of the 10 Mountains of Influence you believe that you are called to.

NOTES……….

_____

_____

_____

_____

_____

_____

_____

_____

_____

_____

_____

Chapter 6 – Promises

Time to Step Forth

Activate your Promises

Life is a Journey and a journey requires a process to get to the destination. God could have birth Christ as a full-grown man, like he did with Adam, but He didn't do that. God allowed Jesus to go through a process to birth forth the promise of re-demption. While God's PROMISES are sure, the process is something He normally does not share. The process is based on the decisions and choices that you make daily, so make sure they are good. God promised me that I would be the mother of three and that one of the three would be a son. What He didn't tell me was that I would have to go through a fight to birth forth that son.

My son was declared dead in my womb. I was hospitalized for weeks. One night, the resident doctor on duty decided that he was going to abort the baby because he thought that there was no life in my womb. It was a good thing that I was familiar with healthcare and knew that I could refuse care. I did that, because while I couldn't feel my son in my womb, I knew by faith that He was alive.

Today this son is eight (8) years old. I had to go through a process to birth forth the promise. God used the process that I went through to help so many other families that had difficulty conceiving or having children to believe again. Through this process, I birth forth and published a book titled, **"Pregnant with a Promise"** that is in high-demand. The book goes into details about losses, and births and what to do when it seems like your dream has died. Do the dreams live again? Yes, they do!

Stand on the word of God, believe by Faith and do the works that's necessary to see your promises manifest. You will need to fight for your prophetic promises. Do not let the enemy win. You already have the VICTORY! Your process could end up being a book, TV Show, Ministry, Conference or a Testimony that's designed to be a blessing to you and to others. I decree and declare that your promises and purpose will not die but will live. Take the necessary steps to not just survive but to thrive and experience your **MEGALIFE**.

 **Moment………………**

What are your Aha moments from this section? What revelation/s did you receive? What will you activate now?

_____

_____

_____

_____

_____

_____

_____

_____

_____

_____

Prayer: Pray for God to re-veal to you His PURPOSE for your life, if you don't already know what it is.

Activation: Review any prophetic words that you have received. Go back through them because God says He's going to re-veal some things that you missed before. It's time for MEGA MANIFESTATIONS.

Chapter 7 – Rosh Hashanah

Head of the Year

On Sunday, September 9, 2018 at sundown, many Jews and Christians started the celebration of one of the Biblical New Year called **Rosh Hashanah** (Hebrew: ראש השנה), which literally means "head of the year." Jewish days start on sundown/sunset and goes until sundown/sunset the next day. In the book of Genesis, when God completed His work for the day, the scripture says, there was evening and there was morning the first day. *"God called the light "day," and the darkness he called "night." And there was evening, and there was morning---the first day."* Genesis 1:5 NIV. So that's why you will tend to see that Hebraic celebrations starts in the evening.

Nevertheless, for simplicity purposes, Rosh Hashanah, New Year 5779 (Ayin Tet – which I will describe in more details), was fully celebrated on September 10, 2018 on the Gregorian calendar. According to Numbers 29:1 AMP

"On the first day of the seventh month on New Year's Day of the civil year, you shall have a holy summoned assembly; you shall do no servile work. It is a day of blowing of trumpets for you everyone blowing who wishes, proclaiming that the glad New Year has come and that the great Day of Atonement and the Feast of Tabernacles are now approaching."

Rosh Hashanah is also the first day of the Highest Holy Holiday or Yamim Noraim ("Days of Awe"), which is celebrated for ten days and leads up to what's called **Yom Kippur**, which I will also discuss later on in the text. **Rosh Hashanah** is observed on the first two days of

Tishrei, which is the seventh (7th) month of the Hebrew calendar. It is described in the Torah as יום תרועה (Yom Teru'ah, a day of sounding [the Shofar]). You're probably wondering why a New Year is celebrated in the 7th month of the year and not the first month in the year. That's because there are two (2) different Hebraic New Year.

There are two (2) New Year on the Hebraic Calendar. One is called the **Civilian New Year** and the other the **Biblical New Year**. The Civilian New Year is **Rosh Hashanah** and is believed to be the time when God created Adam and Eve, thus, it's also the celebration of mankind and creation, thanking God for His Creation and for renewing a good year, every year. In fact, one of the sayings that is said at Rosh Hashanah's corporate and personal worship services is that **"God would renew for us a good year."** The second New Year is Nisan 1 (around March/April) and Nisan is the first (1st) month in the Hebrew Calendar and is considered the Biblical New Year. It's the commemorative of when the children of Israel exiting Egypt – the Great Exodus.

There are also two other minor New Year Tu BiShvat or Tu B'Shevat or Tu B'Shvat (Hebrew: ט"ו בשבט) is a minor Jewish holiday, occurring on the 15th day of the Hebrew month of Shevat (typically January or February on the Gregorian Calendar). It is also called "The New Year of the Trees" or (Hebrew: ראש השנה לאילנות, Rosh HaShanah La'Ilanot). Tu BiShvat is one of four "New Year's" mentioned in the Mishnah. Lastly, a non-celebrated New Year is the 1st day of Elul (August-September) and was celebrated as the tithe of animals when that was a requirement in the early biblical days.

Rosh Hashanah is a time of celebration and feasting and showing gratitude to God for making it to another year. Typically, on Rosh Hashanah, families gather together and feast, have fun and celebrate, just like January 1st in the Gregorian Calendar. Some of the special traditions that take place on Rosh Hashanah are; dipping bread and apples in honey or something sweet.

Our immediate family observes **Rosh Hashanah** as well as the other required feasts. This is one of the most enjoyable time for our children, because they love to bake treats and dip bread and apples in honey. It's just a glorious time and one that all God's people should really partake of because it's required. Taking time to observe the day, tells God that His timing and seasons are more important to you. It also tells Him that you want to have a Good Year and that you need Him to help you have one.

On **Rosh Hashanah**, we do **NOT** work outside of the home as written in Numbers 29:1, "*...you shall do no servile work...*" If it's a school day, our children do not attend school. While it doesn't say that the children should not attend school, it's really a no-brainer. On January 1st, when the parents don't have work, the children also don't have school. Therefore, we follow the same principle.

Since my family and I started observing God's time to the fullest, we have noticed significant blessings in our lives. If you desire to live a life of fullness and joy, then consider meeting up with God for His appointed times. He wants to meet with you. Observing His appointed times comes with many blessings and benefits.

There are **Eight** (8) required Feasts and Festivals:

The Lord's Appointed Times

1. **Sabbath** (Shabbat) – Friday Evening to Saturday Evening
2. **Passover** (Pesach) – 14 Nisan and it's usually around March-April
3. **Unleavened Bread** (Matzo) – 15-21 Nisan (March-April)
4. **FirstFruits to Weeks/Pentecost** (Shavuot) 16 Nisan – 6 Sivan (March-June)
5. **Trumpets (Rosh Hashanah)** – 1 Tishrei (September – October)
6. **Day of Atonement** (Yom Kippur) – 10 Tishrei (September – October)
7. **Booths/Tabernacles** (Sukkot) – 15-21 Tishrei (September – October)
8. **Eighth Day of Rejoicing in the Torah** (Simchat Torah) – 22 Tishrei (September – October)

Added were:
1. **Lots** (Purim) – based around the story of Esther
2. **Dedication** (Hanukah) – also known as the festival of lights
3. **Ninth of Av** (Tisha B'Av) – remembering when the Temple was destroyed.

There are other times and days of observances, but these are the required appointed times as instructed by God that He wants us to remember and teach them to our children so that the traditions continue. **Rosh Hashanah** is such a wonderful time and if you have never experienced the Festival and/or get a chance to blow or hear the blowing of the Shofar, you are missing out. There's an opportunity to partake in the celebration this year on September 30, 2019 with us live. Stay connected with us and you can join us live in person or on the internet for Rosh Hashanah 5780. (Kingdom CiU on Facebook).

Times and Seasons

 *"Teach us to number our days, that we may gain a heart of wisdom."*
Psalm 90:12 NIV

Understanding Times and Seasons and biblical numerology may be insignificant to some, but in Judaism and to Prophets they are more than significant, they represent God's voice and is one of His languages that He communicates with His people. Christians should understand and know God's timing, because numbers have character and reveal many truths, including understanding the **Torah** (first five books of the Bible), also knows as the Pentateuch. It also reveals that **Jesus Christ** is the Messiah and that He was with God, is God and will return for those that have accepted Him as their personal **Lord and Savior** and have lived a holy life.

Understanding God's timing and seasons and being able to rightly divide the word and see and hear what God is saying requires understanding of both the **Hebraic Calendar** and the **Gregorian Calendar**. They work together and form a horizontal (-) and a vertical (l) line which represents the cross (+). Jesus Christ is never missing from what God is doing, because had it not been for Christ, there would be no revelation from the Holy Spirit and mankind would not have direct access to God.

Transitioning to the Hebraic calendar is not an easy process, so I would suggest starting with observing the **Sabbath Day** and **Rosh Hashanah**. However, you can completely partake of all the Appointed Times that were mentioned in the previous section. God looks at the heart and if He sees your desire to understand His timing then He will guide you along the way. You can also start by purchasing a Messianic

Jewish Calendar that shows both the Hebraic and the Gregorian days and months. This is the calendar that I use. Also, if you have an Apple iPhone, you can add the Hebrew Calendar to your existing calendar app and that's a great start. I don't know if the other smart phones have the Hebrew app as I don't own one.

Look at it this way, when you live according to both calendars, you get to enjoy both worlds, and celebrate three (3) New Years; two (2) on the Hebraic Calendar and one (1) on the Gregorian Calendar. Who doesn't like more reasons to celebrate? Furthermore, when one lives according to God's Calendar, he or she understands what season of life they're in, what season the land is in and what to do during each season. It simply brings more meaning to life and removes any anxiety that one may have.

I don't get raveled up or anxious when I see signs and wonders happening around me, because I know that it's just prophesies being fulfilled. We are living in the end times and having a knowledge of the timing will help one to better prepare and embrace what God is doing. Time is advancing, and God is doing some suddenlies. Are you ready to partake with what He's doing?

There are so many mysteries and revelations that are found in the written word of God that has to do with timing, numbers and seasons. For example, the first place in the Bible that the word heal or any variation of healing/health appears is **Genesis 20:17**. Nowhere in the written word of God before Genesis 20, verse 17 will you find the word heal. In the year 2017, I wrote a book called Heal-thy LiFE™, Heal-thy Land that became a best seller (internationally) within one hour of launching it.

God revealed to me and I wrote an entire book about this, that the year 2017 was a year of healing, many victories. While on Tour, we witnessed many healings, miracles, signs and wonders, such as marriages restored, tumors shrinked, cancer healed, the deaf was able to hear and so much more. I've since written the 2nd edition with updated stories and it can be found here:

Https://www.amazon.com/author/carolynganderson

The point is, there are mysteries and hidden revelations in the word of God that will help you understand times and seasons. Before the foundations of the world, God knew that He would reveal the **Year 2017** as the **MVP Year** and the Year of many healings, considering that Genesis 20:17 existed before the beginning of time. God also knew that there would be a Prophet in place that He could reveal His mystery to. God has many revelations that He wants to reveal to you, so it's time to get in position and focus on hearing what God is saying.

 **Moment..........**

One of the missing blessings in most of the Christian community is to truly operate according to God's calendar. Christians will become unstoppable, more powerful and a force to reckon with if they would tap into God's timing and seasons and enjoy the blessings of being truly engrafted into the royal family.

Unfortunately, so many Christians do not know that they have a unique gift by having the ability to live according to the Hebraic and Gregorian calendar. This gives more days to celebrate life and honor God. Time to live in the MEGA!

Numbers & Biblical Numerology

Have you ever read a passage of scripture and noticed that the scripture is repeated? That is not by accident or coincidence, as there's no such thing with God. When God repeats himself, He's making a point. He's really attempting to get our attention to realize that the matter is very important. According to **Genesis 41:32 NIV** Joseph said, **"The reason the dream was given to Pharaoh in <u>two forms</u> is that the matter has been firmly decided by God, and God will do it soon."** There are also times when certain numbers show up frequently, and that is also not coincidental. The bible is the blueprint for life and every answer that one needs can be found there.

Biblical Numerology and numbers are very important, but they are not magic or to be mis-interpreted. Numbers are so significant to God that there's an entire book in the bible titled

Numbers. Biblical Numerology requires interpretation and sound analyzing and understanding from the Holy Spirit. For example, many have read Genesis 20:17, over and over again, including myself, but it wasn't until God was ready to reveal about healing and Gen: 20:17 that it became significant. The scripture existed before you and me, but it had to be the right timing for the revelation. Sometimes understanding the revelation takes time, prayer and fasting. At other times, it helps to ask other Prophets what they are sensing, especially those who God has given the grace and the gift to understand biblical numerology.

 *"My people are destroyed from lack of knowledge."*
Hosea 4:6 NIV

The bible says that we are destroyed from a lack of knowledge and this indeed is true. The lack of knowledge and understanding of God's times and seasons can destroy one's destiny. I was being destroyed when I didn't have the knowledge of God's timing and seasons and now that I know, I do differently. I was alive, but I wasn't truly living.

Everything that God does, the enemy always attempt to create a look alike, but it's always a counterfeit. The enemy has tainted the blessing that comes with true numerology and understanding mysteries and hidden codes in the written word of God. The enemy has twisted it into witchcraft and fortune-telling. He has his own false prophetic team, psychic's and tarot readers, who claim to be able to share future occurrences by reading palms and performing other satanic acts. They even attempt to make economic predictions, but always fail, because truth always trump lies. The enemy's counterfeit will never succeed, because God only reveals His Plans to His servants, the Prophets (Amos 3:7), and not to those who do NOT belong to Him.

I hope the contents in this book bring revelations and enlightenment of the importance of living according to God's timing. God's covenant and His promises belong to those that have chosen Jesus Christ (Yeshua) as Lord and Savior. This is the year to not let the promises pass you by. It's the **MEGA (A-Gem) Year** and God is **Making Everyday Good Again**. Are you ready?

Pause Moment......................

Pause and take a moment and review Chapter 7. Write down what you've learned about **Rosh Hashanah and the Appointed Times**. Reflect on what you've learned about **Times and Seasons**. This moment is all about you. Write down any **Aha moments** or revelations that you received.

_____

_____

_____

_____

_____

_____

_____

_____

_____

_____

_____

Chapter 8 – The Year 5779

Ayin Tet (pronounced like Tate)

Welcome to **Ayin Tet**, the Hebrew Year **5779** – the year of light and the separation of good from evil. It's the year of 2nd Chances and allowing the light in life to shine. It's a year of a FRESH START. As stated before, numbers are very significant to God, whether in the Hebraic or the Gregorian Calendar. On the Hebraic Calendar however, not only do the Years have significant meanings, they have names with numerical values.

Ayin is the 16th letter of the Hebrew alphabet (Aleph-Bet) and represents the numeric value of seventy. Therefore, since the turn of the

70's in the Hebraic Calendar, each year starts off as Ayin plus, (whatever the other numerical value is). For example, last year 5778 (2018) was Ayin-Chet (the number 8), thus, creating seventy-eight (78), using only the two last numbers of the year. This year 5779 is Ayin Tet (the number nine) creating 57-79.

It is similar to describing what the number 19 means for the year 2019. Very rarely the 20 is talked about, but rather the last two numbers. Both the Hebraic and the Gregorian Calendars are coming to an end in its strain. Pretty soon, it will be 57-80 and 20-20, and the re-start of counting of the years 1-9, such as 5781 and 2021. It is going to be a rather interesting and exciting time. I am really excited, because God has already given me instructions and revelations for the upcoming years. God is really doing a new thing in our lives and it's truly an exceptional time to be alive. I hope you are sensing God's love for His People.

Here's an image of the basic Hebrew Alphabet

Image credit: www.hebrew4christians.com

Hebraic Alphabet numbers are easy to understand because it always comes with a pictorial meaning. The pictorial meaning of Ayin (other than 70) is eye and it is used to note vision or insight. Ayin is a letter that also denotes critical points in history and perfect spiritual order.

The word Ayin also represent the **primeval light**, that is the spiritual light of God mentioned in Genesis 1:3, which is different from the celestial light of God mentioned in Genesis 1:14-18. The light mentioned in Genesis 1: 3-4, is Jesus Christ Himself. He is the light of the world and God was calling Christ into being. Light appeared before the objects that produced light (Genesis 1:14-18) existed. God had not yet made the sun, star or the moon.

According to the Jewish midrash, God's spiritual light is far greater than the light from the sun and the stars (www.hebrew4christians.com). This means that during the years of Ayin, any darkness that is hidden in your life, can be broken by decreeing "let there be light" and standing on the word of God. Let the Ayin years of your life be brightened and let your light shine.

The Year of 2nd Chances

 *Tet*

The ninth letter of the Hebrew Alphabet is Tet (sounds like Tate). The pictorial image for Tet resembles a G on its back with a Crown. Some sources have mentioned that it's like a wrapped coiled snake, having both good and evil meaning. I would like to believe that for God's people it represents God crowning us with His Glory. As stated earlier, God had given me the meaning for each year for the next 7 cycles of sevens, so in essence another 49 years. According to (hebrews4christians.com), it states that Tet is a paradoxical letter in that it reveals both good (tov) and evil. The form of the letter is "inverted" suggesting hidden goodness, like that of a woman who is with child.

Tet, spelled backwards is the same word, like Eve, which confirms why this year is a year of 2nd chances. So, it is for the **MEGA** (A-Gem) Year, spelled backwards it's saying that it's a good year. The meaning of Tet is good. The first place **Tet** appears in the Bible is Genesis 1:4, as being a **good** light. "God saw that the light was **good**, and he separated the light from the darkness." There was a reason why God separated the light from the darkness. This is the year where God is separating those who are acting as though they are in Christ and are not. It's also a time for you to separate that which appears to be any form of darkness in your life.

The year **5779** gives you access to activate the 2nd chance of living the **MEGALIFE** one day at a time. Any goals that were not met in 2018, can be achieved in 2019. You have an opportunity to make them become a reality in the #**MEGALiFE** Year.

Pause Moment......................

Pause and take a moment and write down what you have learned about Ayin Tet and the year 5779.

_____

_____

_____

_____

_____

_____

_____

_____

_____

_____

_____

_____

_____

_____

Chapter 9 –Happy New Year

Every January 1st of the Gregorian calendar it's New Year's Day, which is the only New Year that's a part of the Gregorian Calendar, unlike the Hebraic Calendar that has two (2) New Year. It's normally a fun and exciting time and most people seem to be mostly in good spirits. Some will share their goals and aspirations for the new year on social media and other communication outlets. Instead of goals, others will say that they are making new year's resolutions and they seem very confident and proud that this new year will be the year that all things great shall happen.

There are some typical traditions that usually take place during the new year, such as: some people attend a New Year's Eve church service, while others host parties or travel to New York City to see the New Year's Eve ball drop. Some simply stay at home and watch television and bring in the new year with their family.

Lots of weddings and marriage proposals also take place on New Year's Eve/Day and sometimes some break-ups. While there are several festivities and traditions that takes place on January 1st, there are no specific written instructions or guidelines written in the word of God for the celebration of January 1st as there is for Rosh Hashanah or any of the Hebrew New Year.

Therefore, since I am very aware of how important days and times are to God, my immediate family and I have instituted our own traditions for January 1st. We host our Church's New Year's Eve Celebration from 6:30pm to 8:30pm so that the new year is celebrated with family. It's our belief that you should welcome the new year with family and be at home if possible. This is the same tradition that's practiced in Judaism. There's a worship gathering at the temple or at a community center and there's singing, and dancing and the families go home to continue the celebration.

At midnight on New Year's Eve, our family make decrees and declarations that we are expecting to have, such as declaring that it shall be a good year. By December 31st, I would have shared with my family what the New Year is all about, because God usually shares with me the meaning of the year since Rosh Hashanah the preceding year. Our children love the celebrations, because a big part of it includes making treats, having fun, and cooking some of their favorite dishes.

On January 1st, there's a specific process that we follow for goal setting and usually by the end of January we have completed our **Manifestation Maps**™ and are ready to activate the word of the Lord for the year. Personally, for me, one of my goals for the month of January is to finish the book for the year, as I did for this book. Typically, I launch the book for the year by January 31st of the given year. This is also when I start the Tour for the Word of the Lord.

This year **2019** is an extremely historic moment in time, because it's the year when God is **Making Everyday Good Again (MEGA)**. It's the year of separating **Light** from **Darkness** and living a life of Abundance. I hope you are as excited as I am, because it is indeed a **GOOD MEGA YEAR**.

NOTES..........

Chapter 10 –A-Gem (MEGA) Year 2019

Making Everyday Good Again

NOW! The moment that you have been waiting for. It's time for the great reveal of what this **#MEGA YEAR** is all about. I have been anticipating writing this chapter because it is so **MEGA.** This is the year when God is Making Everyday Good Again. This is absolutely one of the best years ever and yes, you have probably heard that before, but hopefully from reading the previous chapters, you have noticed that seasons, times and days, all belong to God and that it's very important to him that you embrace his New

Movement. This is truly the year of 2nd chances and a year of the overflow. As Bishop T.D. Jakes would say "get ready, get ready, get ready."

The year **2019** is the **MEGA** year and if you haven't figured it out yet, the acronym **MEGA** stands for **Making Everyday Good Again.** Last year **MEGA** was for **Making Everything Good Again and it surely was**. Everything God made is and was good and everyday He made is and was good. This is the year when God is taking us back to **Genesis** for those who will participate in the **MEGALiFE** Movement. Everything God made, He saw that it was good and if everything He made was good then every day that He also made is a good day, because only goodness comes from the Father.

Everyday should be a day of expecting Good-News, because since Christ was with God in the beginning, it means that everything, every day, every life, every moment in God, are all good. According to Genesis 1:18 NIV, it says that *"...And God saw that it was good."* First God spoke *"let there be"* and then He saw that what He created was good. You are God's good creation and you're living in a good time. Just like God, one has to speak (declare) what you want to see in your life and that's how you will see the manifestation in your life.

In the year 2017 – the **MVP Year**, God completed most of His resetting, because things and people's lives had gotten out of control. This was not God's first reset and it probably won't be His last before the return of Christ. However, 2017 was a year of the Re's. Reset's are significant because it allows things to start new and fresh again. In the book of Acts,3:19, 21, NIV, it describes how God is always restoring and refreshing. He does this, because again, it is NOT God's will that anyone should perish.

> *"Repent, then, and turn to God, so that your sins may be wiped out, that times of refreshing may come from the Lord, Heaven must receive him until the time comes for God to **restore everything**, as he promised long ago through his holy prophets."*

Reset's are not new set of phenomenon's as they are clearly written in the Word of God. Reset's can be personal, geographical, cultural or even global. A very specific global and obvious reset took place during the days of Noah, when God created a **new beginning** after the flood. This is one of the reasons why the number eight (8) is said to be the number of new beginnings. God started mankind all over again with eight people, namely; Noah and his wife, their three (3) sons and their wives. They were the chosen family during that timeframe that God made all things new again. He washed away all the corruption and sin, because He can only tolerate foolishness for so long. God is the same God then, today and forevermore and once again, God is instituting a new beginning.

Another major reset was the death and resurrection of Jesus Christ. God sent His Son to die for you and me, that through Him, we would be restored, redeemed and be engrafted back into God's family. Mankind was heading in the wrong direction, and Christ became the pause moment, the RESET, that would give us life again. Due to His redemptive power, there's a new start, a new beginning, an upgraded life. God used 2017 as a year that He performed some resets in people's lives and prophetically, there were three (3) major resets that I wrote about in the book **(2017 The MVP Year)**. It was imperative that these resets took place to get things and lives back in order. These resets needed to happen to prepare for 2018, 2019 and the **MEGALiFE** Movement.

MEGA *Making Everyday Good Again*

There are also natural resets, such as new leadership positions, new presidents, new seasons and so forth that all took place and probably will continue to take place. I wrote about the Remnants and a changing of the guards earlier in the text. God is handing the baton to the people and the generation that should be in leadership positions today. Not all leaders effectively passed the baton. Some of them held on to it, even to their graves. Again, God's will must always be done, and if He has to move people out of the way so that His plans continue, then that's what He will do.

Recently, I purchased a new iPhone and it started experiencing some problems. The technician instructed me to reset the phone so that it can be restored to its original state with new software. After I followed this process, the phone started working much better and the problems were resolved. This is what a reset is all about. It allows things to become new all over again, with upgrades and improvement so that things can work the way they should. God is doing some major upgrades and those who are alive will get to see the manifestations of it! It's the **MEGA** Year, It's **A-Gem** Year.

Now that the major resets are over, God is re-establishing His order and making everyday good again. I used to thing that **Great** was a better word than Good, until I heard a Pastor say that the ultimate disposition of God is Him being a **Good God**. This helped me to understand why in the book of Genesis, after God made everything, He **saw** that it was good and not that it was great. It's not that greatness is not an awesome state, because it is, but there's a reason why God said it was good and not that it was great. God's best is when He say it is **Good**. Making Everyday Good Again is both a spiritual and a natural new beginning. Just think, every day, every month, every quarter, every season, every year, is an opportunity for you to experience and walk in God's goodness. I speak newness into every area of your life.

There are six (6) times in the first Chapter of Genesis that **God** saw that what He made was **good** and one (1) time **very good** to total seven (7) times, which represents completion and His divine perfection. The following verses describes God's vision of Him seeing everything He made as being good:

Genesis 1:1,4,10,12,18,21,25,31 NIV

"In the beginning God created the heavens and the earth. [4] God saw that the light was **good**, and he separated the light from the darkness. [10] God called the dry ground "land," and the gathered waters he called "seas." And God saw that it was **good**. [12] The land produced vegetation: plants bearing seed according to their kinds and trees bearing fruit with seed in it according to their kinds. And God saw that it was **good**. [18] to govern the day and the night, and to separate light from darkness. And God saw that it was **good**. [21] So God created the great creatures of the sea and every living thing with which the water teems and that moves about in it, according to their kinds, and every winged bird according to its kind. And God saw that it was **good**. [25] God made the wild animals according to their kinds, the livestock according to their kinds, and all the creatures that move along the ground according to their kinds. And God saw that it was **good**. [31] God saw all that he had made, and it was **very good**. And there was evening, and there was morning---the sixth day."

In the beginning, God made the following:

Day 1: Let there be Light!

Day 2: Sky (Separated the waters above from the waters below)

Day 3: Fruits, Vegetables and Trees

Day 4: Sun, Moon, Stars

Day 5: Fish and Birds

Day 6: Animals and Mankind

Day 7: He rested (Sabbath Day)

As God began to reveal to me the complete meaning of the #**MEGA**. He kept saying "all things new." This is the year to speak newness and light into your life. Anytime something old or past things attempt to re-surface in your life, declare that "all things are new." Declare "let there be light." Anything that is dark or not clear, should not be in your life. If you see darkness showing up in your life, don't accept it, instead reject it.

Personally, I was planning to get another used (new to me) vehicle to replace the one that I have now, and God said, nope "all things new." Do not get a used vehicle but get one that is brand new. He didn't' have to tell me twice, I said "okay Lord." This means that God will be providing financial provision so that I can buy the new vehicle with cash, because I don't plan on financing anything in the **MEGA** Year or ever, unless it's a strategic reason, like business credit.

One of the new things that God showed me, was that there shall be many marriages, and re-marriages, new homes, new purchases, new friends, new career, new levels of anointing's, new gifts, new territories and new relationships and so forth. There shall be many things new in 2019 and beyond.

 *"In the beginning was the Word, and the Word was with God, and the Word was God. He was with God from the beginning."*
John 1:1-2 NIV

God is making all things new and pure as it was in the beginning. There was an increase of darkness like it was in the beginning and during all the reset periods. Now God is saying, let there be light. Whenever light shows up in your life, it can only be good. Light exposes darkness and light brings life. Jesus Christ is the light of the world and when He's in your life, there can be no darkness.

God took His time and created all that is needed for mankind to survive. He gave fruits, vegetables, trees, fishes, animals, plants and light. He provided instructions about what to eat and what not to eat. All things were good in the beginning. Life was pure and communication with God was good. The bible says that God communed with Adam in the cool of the day. It would have continued down that path, had sin not became a part of Adam and Eve's life.

The choice they made changed the trajectory of their offspring. Christ had to be sent to redeem mankind because He was with God and is God and knows first-hand about God's divine plan. Now God is redeeming us again, and this time, He's starting all over and making everyday good again. God loves us so much that He has chosen **to have us experience a FRESH START,** a new beginning of making our day brand new again. This is NOT new to God, as everyday is a new day, however, it wasn't declared in the Earth as it requires a Prophet to establish God's Plan and be His Voice.

Part of the process of making things new requires a separation of light and darkness. There will be a difference between those who are of the light and those who represent darkness. There is no getting around this in the #**MEGA** Year and the #**MEGA** Cycle.

Light vs. Darkness

"God saw that the light was good, and he separated the light from the darkness."

Genesis 1:4 NIV

Everything in life is a process. From the foundations of the world God created the heaven's and the earth by applying a process. According to Genesis 1:1-3, it says:

"In the beginning God created the heavens and the earth. Now the earth was formless and empty, darkness was over the surface of the

deep, and the Spirit of God was hovering over the waters. And God said, "Let there be light," and there was light."

God will be separating light from darkness. Those who are on the fence or in the middle (lukewarm), will need to choose to be hot or cold, in the light or in darkness. There are some who call themselves Christians but are living according to the world's standard of life. Christianity is more than attending church or being a part of the choir. It is an everyday lifestyle and the light should shine in everything that a Christian does. Christians should be living an abundant life, always having more than enough and never living below God's standards.

God has been very patient, and He has given many, an opportunity to get it right. He has extended extra Grace (it seems) during 2015 and 2016 - the Spin Cycle Years and in 2017 - the Reset Year. He even had a year where things were simply just up and down in 2018. He doesn't want to see His creation perish. He wants to see everyone saved and live prosperously, but we all know that not everyone will be saved based on the choices he or she makes.

Unfortunately, the decision of whether or not one perishes or don't is contingent on choices that each person make. Consequently, it's not too late. There's always an opportunity for repentance and forgiveness, always. However, there comes a point when God has to separate light from darkness. It is inevitable. There came a point when He had to destroy Sodom and Gomorrah and started a new lifestyle for Lot and his family. Once again God is now looking for those who are ready to live life fully every day, forever, and be His Ambassadors for the Kingdom.

Infinity

MEGA also means infinity, a never-ending source of provision. It's creating a new economy, that never runs dry. **MEGA** represents infinite blessings, abundance, overflow and **always having more than enough**. The number represents everything that is ultimately good and because it has no ending point, it demonstrates that it's a continuous blessing. It is a divine number that also represents vision. This type of vision is being able to see with the mind and not with the eyes. It is a profound number because it's the number that God uses for new beginnings. After He created the heavens and the earth in six (6) days, and rested on the Sabbath (Seventh) day, the eighth (8th) day was the day of new beginnings. This is the season to focus on God's infinite blessings. It's the beginning of a new life for His chosen ones, welcome to the MEGALiFE!

Chapter 11 - Palace Time

Image Credit: Joshua Ivan Sudrajat

Life is a Journey filled with seasons, cycles and TIME. Seasons exist within cycles and cycles exist within TIME. Seasons are cycles or cyclical, but TIME is Constant and Dimensional. For example, when Joseph went to live in the Palace it was his time to rule and reign. Yet his time would be broken down into 7-year cycles, which were the **Seven years of Abundance** and 7 years of famine. Within those seven years, each year had 4 different seasons and each season, had months, weeks, days, hours and seconds. However, no matter what season or cycle Joseph was going through, once he entered the **PALACE** he stepped into the season of Time. This was when his true purpose manifested. Joseph remained in the palace for the rest of his life. This is when life shifts to a new level and one starts living in TIME. Decree that when you have entered or is entering your Palace Season, that you will NOT go back to the old ways of living.

This is the **#MEGA YEAR** when God is **Making Everyday Good Again**. He doesn't desire for you to be complacent, stagnant, depressed, broken or broke. Instead, His desire is that you would prosper and be in good health. He desires that you will be filled with joy, happiness, peace and contentment. While God's will and desire for your life is good, it doesn't mean that it is automatic. For example, it's God's will that none would perish. However, some will perish. That's because God's will for our lives is contingent on the choices that are made daily.

God creates our destiny, but we choose our path. If you want this **MEGA** life bad enough, then prove it to God, by provoking His will. Show Him the urgency. Let Him see the desperation of Making Everyday Good Again. This is how you will attract the MEGA life into being. Let you desire match your action.

The time has come when you can use your gifts and talents that God gave you to take your rightful place in His Kingdom. In one of my books "**From the Pit to the Palace**, I share that all life's experiences that we go through is to get us tough enough and equipped to lead like Joseph had to, so he can see the manifestations of God's promises. God always have an appointed time for everything and no man or devil can stop it. God's set and appointed time to live the **MEGA** life and enter the **PALACE season and TIME** is at hand.

Wealth Transfer

"And I will make the Egyptians favourably disposed toward this people, so that when you leave you will not go empty handed."

Exodus 3:21 NIV

Since the time of Exodus from EGYPT, there has not been a major transfer of Wealth for God's People. This also means that since the time when Christ was on earth and ascended there hasn't been a major WEALTH TRANSFER either. The transfer is overdue. According to Exodus 3:20-22 NIV it states *"So I will stretch out my hand and strike the Egyptians with all the wonders that I will perform among them. After that, he will let you go. "And I will make the Egyptians favorably disposed toward this people, so that when you leave you will not go empty-handed. Every woman is to ask her neighbor and any woman living in her house for articles of silver and gold and for clothing, which you will put on your sons and daughters. And so, you will plunder the Egyptians."*

This major Wealth Transfer requires a process just like it was during the Exodus. God has already started the process that's needed for the WEALTH transfer. First, He did some cleansing in 2016, many victories and healing in 2017, fresh start in 2018 and now a 2nd chance to step into a Wealthy Place. It's time for the unhealthy life to EXODUS. It's time for it to go! You can have complete wealth in all areas of your life. Wealth is more than finances, considering that "True Wealth starts with your Health in mind." The Wealth Transfer is overdue.

WEALTH was transferred to Joseph because he went through the **process** that led to him walking out his PURPOSE. Purpose is a journey and not a final destination. Joseph went from being chosen, the most favored son to being in slavery, accusation and prison. From there he was promoted to the Palace. Your prayers are about to be answered. God is saying that as you prepare yourself in this season, where your GIFT makes room for you and in no time, you shall reap what you have sown.

In Acts 12:12-16 NIV, while the people were praying for Peter to be released from Prison, an Angel of the Lord released Peter and he went and knocked at the door to announce his release. God is releasing you from your pain, suffering, prison season and from debt because you've knocked at the door and it's time for it to be OPENED.

The major transfer will take place when you STEP into your PURPOSE. What were you created to be? Just like anything in life there's a process to get to the result. Moses had to go through a process to redeem the children of Israel. David had to walk through a process to rule in the palace. I had to go through a process to get to where I am today and so shall you.

Get ready! You are about to experience a major Wealth Transfer if you have been in position and prepared for it. Get ready for the overnight promotions from the Prison season to the Palace season. Walk in your year of the **MEGALiFE™**, in your year of light, and the year of 2nd chances. It's time to Awaken your life and live the best life you've ever lived. Now is not the time to fall asleep or to let others pass you by. Now is not the time for you to be burdened down with problems, depression, confusion or despair. It's the time to rejoice. It's the time to shout. It's the time to take down all the giants in your life and be awakened.

NOTES..........

Take a moment and reflect on Chapter 11 and journal the journey. What season of life do you believe you are in?

_____

_____

_____

_____

_____

_____

_____

_____

_____

_____

_____

Chapter 12 – The Awakening

"Awake, harp and lyre! I will awaken the dawn."
Psalm 108:2 NIV

For the last few years, I have been hearing stories of revivals and awakenings and a great big change that's coming. My husband and I are very familiar with awakenings as we've been ministering about the awakening for the last seven (7) years. The great BIG change that Prophets have been declaring that's coming, is actually here NOW. Since one of the gifts of the Prophet is to foretell and to see ahead of time, what can happen is, they continue to declare what's coming and don't see that what they were saying is coming, is actually here. Their prophecies were fulfilled and now it's time to lead the people in the manifestation of the prophecies. It's time to strategize and work the prophecies, per se.

God released an awakening strategy that you can participate in. He has already qualified and equipped you to pursue your rightful position in the Kingdom. According to Colossians 1:2 AMP *"Giving thanks to the Father, Who has qualified and made us fit to share the portion which is the inheritance of the saints (God's holy people) in the Light."* Therefore, the time is now for you to activate your influence and maximize what you have been gifted to carry out. Earth needs you to occupy your space and pursue your purpose and take dominion.

THE AWAKENING STRATEGY

- ✓ **Apostles** – The anointing of an Apostle is to plant, build and re-build churches, ministries, cities, nations and families. Apostles are responsible for being overseer's and leading leaders.

- ✓ **Prophets** - laying the foundation and being the leading voice that God uses to establish His Plans. It's more than bringing a prophetic word to the people. It's about being a leader and working together to re-build God's foundation. They are to travel and prophesy what thus says the Lord and not necessarily be in the four (4) walls of the local church.

- ✓ **Evangelist** - spreading the word of God on the highways and byways, going into homes and ministering the word of God. Stirring up the spirit of God in the people. True Evangelism is about going into the world. It's not necessarily about preaching in the church, but rather sharing the Good-News to those who are lost.

- ✓ **Pastors** - ministering to the people, being a shepherd over the sheep. Pastor of different groups to those assigned to them. Oftentimes the leader of a congregation is referred to as the Pastor and while that may last for a service time, it becomes overwhelming if that congregation has over 50 people. It will become chaotic and out of order. When there were multitudes that needed to be fed, Jesus instructed His disciples to have the people sit down in groups of fifty, Luke 9:14. The Pastor cannot shepherd the people, acts as the administrator and is expected to bring a weekly sermon that will impact and inspire the lives of the congregants. This is not possible and that is why so many congregations seem (dead) and stagnant, because the people aren't growing. Therefore, it's time to separate the congregation with multiple Pastors who lead different groups and having overseers such as Apostles and Prophets that help to build up the church and teachers that teach.

- ✓ **<u>Teachers</u>** - rightly dividing the word. Teaching the Word of God for understanding and revelation.

- ✓ **<u>Revivals</u>** – hosting revivals for the saints (can't revive something that was never birth) focus on reviving the Christians or the backsliders.

- ✓ **<u>Missionaries</u>** - going on a mission to help the sick, poor and the homeless and visiting those in hospitals. Helping the orphans, widows and those less fortunate. Missionaries are not to be in the four walls preaching. This is where they come to be re-fueled. A Missionary is a full-time work and so you should have systems set up in place that provides financial support as you go on the journey.

- ✓ **Intercessors and Prayer Warriors-** praying strategic prayers until they see breakthrough. Intercessors are so powerful and can be sometimes an overlooked group. They carry the heart of God and have a special place in His heart. They are one of the most needed ministries in Christendom today.

- ✓ **Gifts** - Each Christian using their gifts and talents in the KINGDOM (whether marketplace or in the physical church).

- ✓ **Adopt a Block** -**Transform a City** going into the neighborhoods to clean (one block at a time) build trust, show and tell (show God by loving the un-loving and helping the less fortunate and then tell Christ). Provide basic human needs first and then share the good news.

- ✓ **Chaplains** - Police Chaplains, Disaster Chaplains, Sex & Human Trafficking etc. Marketplace Chaplains working full time in Corporate firms.

- ✓ **Safe Havens/Group Homes** - homes for the poor, widow, abused, lost, homeless, broken. Christian's purchasing the homes and turning them into shelters or group homes.

- ✓ **Workplace Chaplains** - getting into the workplace and becoming a part of the leadership team. Go on the inside as an undercover so that he or she can become an influencer and make moral and godly decisions that affects the people.

The Ten (10) Spheres of Influence
Similar to the 7 Mountains + 3

1. **Businesses** - supporting Christian led businesses. Starting your own business. Becoming the next CEO, Leader, Executive etc. **Only** use your money to purchase and support companies that you believe in and has the same values as you do.

2. **Arts/Entertainment** - Christian Entertainment, Songs and Music for the NOW GENERATION that edifies GOD. Talk Shows and Public Figures that represents Christ. Going into the Arts and having your talents and skills to demonstrate creativity.

3. **Family** – restoring Kingdom Families, Getting the fathers back into the homes, Marriages between one man and one woman, protecting the entity of family, and standing for justice.

4. **Government** - praying for the leaders. Become a government official or politician yourself so that you can be the decision maker and perhaps the next president of the nation where you reside. Laws that protect families and matters important to Christians. Getting into the systems and becoming the next government officials.

5. **Education** – building our own Kingdom Schools, where the children are taught biblical history and learn who they are at an early age. We need prayer back into the schools and for someone to take the mantle and fight to get back prayers in schools. We need real Kingdom Universities and Colleges, that are teaching economic principles from a biblical perspective.

6. **Religion/Ministry** – it's time to break down the boundaries and barriers of religion that have left many people bound. Man-made rules and regulations have taken the place of sound biblical teaching and have pushed many away from the church. It's time to bring the prodigals back and teach and show them true love, because God is love. Churches will not look the way that it always has, as there's a new way to have church that's being birth right now.

7. **Media** – Time to share the GOOD NEWS! It is time for us to not implode our homes with all the negativity that's happening in and around the world, but to have more Christian news stations, sharing and spreading the good that's happening in the world. We can do this! It's time for Kingdom Citizens to go into the world of Media and be an Ambassador for God.

8. **Science & Technology** – the technological world is different from media. Media is an outlet (whether social media of broadcast television), but technology exist in every area

of life. Whether it is drones, or the latest smart phone, or the ability to go paperless and be all digital, technology is its own spheres of influence. Are you called to that area? Are you called to dominate a space in the technological field? Look at Facebook and Amazon and other products and companies, they are making millions, from a simple vision, an idea, a concept and today they are living the dream. You can do the same.

9. **Healthcare** – this sphere of influence is what I refer to as the undercover secret agent. From working in healthcare on the insurance side, I know first-hand some of what goes on behind closed doors. There's also healthcare on the clinical side, such as hospitals and clinics. The healthcare mountain per se is one of the most influential spheres of influence. One cannot survive without their health, right? Most medications were not intended to get you well, because how else would the pharmaceutical companies make money? They were intended to keep you coming back (maintenance drugs are what they are called). There are some that are necessary but shouldn't be a lifetime dependency. Nevertheless, there are good things that happen and can happen within this sphere, such as scientists researching for the

latest breakthrough cure. Wellness Coaches helping people become better. Are you called to be a doctor, a wellness coach, a fitness instructor and the like? There's healing for every disease. By His Stripes we are healed. Therefore, you can minister healing to see families become whole.

10. **Finance** – While Finance exist within all the Spheres of Influence, the 10 Mountains, considering that money is needed for everything, it's still necessary to be its own mountain because there are people that are gifted with the ability to understand finance and commerce. Are you called to open up a Credit Union and have the money being managed in your system? What about the banking industry, do you see yourself being the head of some of the financial institutions? What about being a prophetic financial advisor, where you can predict the stock market and guide God's people about creating profitable portfolios? There're so many opportunities in any of the area.

These are just some examples of ways that you can occupy your space and walk out your purpose in life. More than likely your purpose falls within one of those spheres of influence above. Therefore, it's time for you to **OCCUPY** your space and use your gift to make room for you and others. You were born to lead.

NOTES..........

Time to Pause…and use the space below to write down what you have learned from this Chapter. What will you apply immediately? What were some aha moments for you? What did you learn that you didn't know before? Which of the Ten (10) spheres of influence do you believe you are called to? Note, it could be more than one.

Summary

 *"...And God saw that it was good."*
Genesis 1:18 NIV

Whew! What a good book! Wow! This is such an impactful book that I will personally read it over again and again. God's voice is permeating earth through the insights and revelations that He gave in this text. I suggest that you go back through and read this again. Similar to the Bible, when you read it again, there's always fresh revelations after the 2nd or 3rd time of reading the text. It was a difficult book for me to write, not because writing is difficult, but because of some of the deep insights and revelations that I was getting, and I had to decide what to include now, and what to include in later books.

Nevertheless, you have more than enough content in this text to last you more than a year. I know that this book will be another best-seller, because of its practically and accuracy. People are looking for a change, a fresh start, a new beginning and they're wanting to hear what God is saying right now. God is speaking very clear. The only way to hear God is to clear the clutter from your mind and focus on what He's telling you to do. If any of the content in this text was a confirmation to something that God or another Prophet told you, then you no longer need to be praying about it, but rather to activate it, because it serves as a witness to you.

The book started off by introducing you to the **MEGA** Year and giving you Background Information about Dr. Carolyn and about the previous years and why God is doing what He's doing now. The purpose of the book was shared so that you have a clear understanding of what this book is all about. It's one thing to be introduced to a text, but without purpose, one does not know where he or she is going.

The Preface included a look-back at the Spin Cycle and the Reset Years. It was necessary to share this as a precursor to what God is doing today, after all, today is all we have. Chapter One goes into specific details about the Spin Cycle **2016** and how God had to squeeze some heaviness out of His people in preparation for the **MVP Year of 2017, leading up to 2019**.

This book then introduced you to the Hebraic Calendar and provided a broad overview of the year 5779. It shared the differences between the Hebraic Calendar and the Gregorian Calendar and how God uses both calendars to execute and establish His Plans. In essence, God's people are in this world but not of this world, meaning that, while we understand that the world has its own system and standards we are keenly aware of who's standard to live by.

There's a new leadership arising. They are the ones that God has given authority to lead in this time. We are called the **REMNANTS** as mentioned in Genesis 45:7.

Chapter Five (5) was what I called one of the **<u>defining moments chapter</u>** as it helps to bring clarity about one's purpose. This is a huge part of living the **MEGALiFE**. The late Dr. Myles Munroe said**, "The greatest tragedy in life is not death, but life without meaning, without a purpose."**

Therefore, it's time to truly live life with meaning. It's important to know where you fit in, within the Ten spheres of influence, also referred to as the ten mountains. It is a great time to be alive and to experience all that God has in store for you. Who would have thought that we would be alive to see the year Twenty Nineteen (2019) and the year 5779?

Are there promises that you are looking to be fulfilled in this **MEGA** Year? If so, review those promises. A big part of the promises manifesting is to understand times and seasons. Life is so much simpler and more peaceful when one knows what season of life he or she is in. It starts and end when God says so.

God started a new season, a new era, a new year called Rosh Hashanah. This is the Civilian Hebraic New Year, when it is said to be when God created Adam and Eve. It is a highly celebrated day by Jews and non-Jews and should be one that is celebrated for all God's people. The Year 5779 is called Ayin Tet, which is a good year and a year of 2nd Chances.

This is the **MEGA** Year, where God is Making Everyday Good Again in Him. It's time to experience the BIG things. Stop playing small as God is a great Big God and He wants to give you great big things and a good life. God is removing any darkness from your life, so that you can experience His Light. It's time to speak "let there be light." It's time to declare your Wealth Transfer and your Palace TIME.

It's time to participate in the Awakening Strategy and stand on your Mountain of Influence. Are you called to occupy your space and activate your purpose to help Families? Are you called to the mountain of Education, Religion or Ministry, Government or Civic Duty, Arts & Entertainment, Business, Media, Healthcare, Science & Technology or Finance? This should be a very clear and specific answer. By now you should know where you believe you would be the most influential and effective.

One doesn't have to like the mountain to occupy it, in fact, the mountain you may be called to, is probable one that you don't like and that's why you'll be the one to make the change in that area. God is using that dislike so that you can be the difference-maker. I don't necessarily like the MEDIA Mountain, because it's too political, very expensive and somewhat corrupt. However, I know why God assigned me to that mountain and He's gracefully giving me strategies of how to navigate through it effectively.

It's time for God's people to stop fussing and arguing about what he or she doesn't like and do something about it. This is what the **MEGA** Year is about. It's time to **AWAKEN** the warrior within you. It's time to be all that God has called, chosen and created you to be and to do. The time is NOW!

Benefits of Decreeing and Declaring

"Thou shalt also decree a thing, and it shall be established unto thee: and the light shall shine upon thy way."

Job 22:27 KJV

I believe that you are ready and fired up to be a difference maker and to decree and declare what thus says the Lord. One of the benefits that's outlined in this text, is that it has **79** declarations that you can use to decree and declare and activate the **MEGA** in your life. One of the questions I get asked, is how do I know what to decree and declare? What scriptures do I speak over my life? What are the right words to use to command my day that aligns with what God is doing and saying? Well, here are the answers. They are clearly written for you. You can use these 79 declarations along with any other text in the word of God to decree over your life or situation.

As you prepare to audibly speak the **79** declarations or any other biblical decrees, please know that there is a pre-requisite that must take place. To receive these benefits, you must first be a son or daughter of the Highest. One of the gifts of being a child of God is that you get complete access to **ALL** His Benefits.

According to Psalm 103:2-14,17-19,22 NIV *"Praise the Lord, my soul, and forget not all his benefits--- who forgives all your sins and heals all your diseases, who redeems your life from the pit and crowns you with love and compassion, who satisfies your desires with good things so that your youth is renewed like the eagle's. The Lord works righteousness and justice for all the oppressed. He made known his ways to Moses, his deeds to the people of Israel: The Lord is compassionate and gracious, slow to anger, abounding in love. He will not always accuse, nor will he harbor his anger forever; he does not treat us as our sins deserve or repay us according to our iniquities. For as high as the heavens are above the earth, so great is his love for those who fear him as far as the east is from the west, so far has he removed our transgressions from us. As a father has compassion on his children, so the Lord has compassion on those who fear him; for he knows how we are formed, he remembers that we are dust. But from everlasting to everlasting the Lord's love is with those who fear him, and his righteousness with their children's children---with those who keep his covenant and remember to obey his precepts. The Lord has established his throne in heaven, and his kingdom rules over all. Praise the Lord, all his works everywhere in his dominion. Praise the Lord, my soul."* When you belong to God you have access to all these benefits and more. He becomes your Healer, Provider, Lawyer, Protector and so much more.

Years ago, my father had prostate cancer and he underwent surgery to remove the cancer. For about two years everything was fine, and it appeared that my dad was cured or in remission as some call in. Tragically the cancer came back or came back from hiding and this time it was more potent and powerful than the first time. His doctors pretty much said that there was nothing else they could do for him. He was just told to get regular checkups and hope that something changed. Thus, his disease became a death sentence.

One Sunday after I ministered at our church service, I extended an open invitation for salvation and to my surprise my dad came to the altar. Growing up, I never saw my dad attend church, but he always made sure that he sent us to church. The only time I saw him at a church service was at a funeral and even there, he hung outside the church. We grew up in Jamaica and it was mostly over 80 degrees so being outside was never a problem for him or anyone that wanted to be outside.

One particular Sunday, I believed my dad was the last person that I prayed for. Prior to praying for him, I asked my dad if he was saved. I asked him if he had ever received Jesus Christ as his personal Lord and Savior. He had not, so then I asked him if he would like to be saved? Without hesitation, he said yes.

After my father accepted Jesus Christ as his savior, I did something I have never done before. I looked directly at my father and said, "it is illegal for two spirits to dwell in the same body, therefore I command the spirit of cancer to leave his body now, because the Holy Spirit now lives there." The following day was one of my dad's regular checkups to check the cancer levels in his body. Long story short, to their amazing surprise there was **<u>no cancer</u>**.

There's nothing too hard for God and when you have accepted His Son it gives you direct access to receive all the benefits from Him. It's no different from places of employment. Upon being hired or even before, one of the things that's shared are benefits that comes with being a part of the organization. So, it is when you are in Christ Jesus, there are benefits that comes with being a part of the kingdom and the pre-requisite is your confession and receiving Jesus Christ as your personal Lord and Savior, like my dad.

Are you ready to live life fully every day? If you are not saved, have turned away from the faith, or just not sure, you now have the opportunity to be saved. If you are already saved, then congratulations, you have everything needed to Decree and Declare.

Confession

It's a simple process that takes less than 5 minutes. It's a three-step process as easy as ABC!

1. Accept Jesus Christ as your Lord and Savior by saying out of your mouth that you accept the Lord as your Personal Savior.
2. Declare audibly that you believe in your heart that Jesus Christ died for you and that He is the risen savior that will return.
3. Confess your sins and ask him to forgive you and you should also forgive others that you need to forgive.

Congratulations! If you have just accepted Jesus Christ as your personal Lord & Savior, you can now fully participate in the blessings that are in store for you.

Date of Salvation: _____

NOTES..........

Journal the Journey

79 Decrees & Declarations

It is time to decree and declare. Start off by saying "This is the day that the Lord has made, we shall rejoice and be glad in it. Every good and perfect gift comes from God—therefore this year is both good and perfect because it comes from God!"

The year 2019 is the MEGA (A-Gem) Year. It's the Year of light, the year to decree, and the year of Abundance. It's the year of the **MEGALiFE™**. It is a year when promises will be fulfilled, a year of goodness and one where many souls will be brought to the Kingdom of God. It's time for an awakening in your life and in the land.

A year of signs, miracles and wonders, a year of prosperity for the righteous ones, a year when God's people shall rule and reign and inherit the earth, by being owners and lenders, and never borrowers. **BELIEVE IT & RECEIVE IT!** This is the **MEGA** Year. Decree it and Declare it.

1. <u>Making Everyday Good Again</u>
2. **Making Everything Good Again**
3. **Making Everything (Earth) Great Again**
4. **Making Everything in Great Abundance**
5. **Making Earth in Great Abundance**
6. **Making Exercising Good Again**
7. **Make Eating Good Again**
8. **Make Earnings Grow Again (Always)**
9. **Multiplying Every-day Good Again**
10. **Making Economy be in Great Abundance**
11. **Making Every Goal Achievable**
12. **Making ENTERTAINMENT Good Again**
13. **Making Employment in Great Abundance**
14. **Multiplying Earth's Good Economy**
15. **Making Entrepreneurship Grow Again**
16. **Making Everyone Give Again**
17. **Making Everyone Glad Again**
18. **Making Expectations Grand Again**
19. **Making Earth Godly Again**

I decree and declare that:

1. This year 2019 is the MEGA Year and the Year to Make Everyday Good Again. It's the Year of New Beginnings and the year of Manifestations, Elevation, Greatness and Abundance
2. This year of our lives will bring divine opportunities that WE will take full advantage of
3. This year is filled with wonderful surprises, supernatural breakthroughs, and miracles from Heaven
4. Today marks the end of a SAD (Standard Adult Day), depressing, discouraging past and the beginning of a prosperous, debt-free, disease-free, depression-free, happy future
5. God will grant us strategies for a prosperous and successful life
6. This year our Prayers will be answered SUDDENLY
7. We will Dance, Shout and Sing to the King
8. We will give more, because we HAVE MORE
9. Our minds will be filled with the knowledge of God's identity
10. We are empowered to accomplish that which we were born to do
11. You are all you were born to be

12. Every day of our lives is in sync with the perfect will of God
13. Our vision is clear
14. Our intentions are pure
15. His WILL BE DONE ON EARTH AS IT IS IN HEAVEN
16. Our relationships are healthy
17. Our minds are healthy
18. Our Finances Are Healthy
19. Our Faith is Healthy
20. Our God supplies all our needs according to His riches in glory
21. We live in a prosperous and healthy environment and we have GREAT NEIGHBORS
22. God has affirmed who we are
23. We are the light of the world and so we shall SHINE

I decree and declare:

24. Joy, peace, prosperity, and success belongs to us
25. We have healthy friendships and are connected to the right people
26. We are filled with Love for God and for each other
27. We have healthy family members
28. We shall use our gifts and they will make room for us

29. We have found FAVOR with God and with man
30. We walk in divine delegated authority and we are the head and not the tail
31. We are world changers and Kingdom Builders
32. We will live a legacy and leave a legacy
33. We have an inheritance from our Heavenly Father and we will leave an inheritance for our future generations.
34. We are renewed and revived
35. We walk in greatness and our brilliance radiates daily
36. We will GLORIFY the GREAT KING
37. We are creative beings and we will live a creative life
38. We are millionaires
39. We are Royalty and unique

I decree and declare that:
40. Our minds are healthy and strong
41. We have a CLEAR VISION of our Future
42. We have the Wisdom of Solomon to make wise choices
43. We will pursue and recover all
44. Restoration belongs to us
45. The blessings of the Lord are upon us and we are rich
46. WE are healthy in our minds, body, soul and spirit

47. We are VICTORIOUS
48. We will no longer STRUGGLE, but will THRIVE
49. OUR enemies are subdued
50. WE ARE fruitful in all OUR endeavors
51. WE have at least 7 streams of income
52. We are the head and not the tail
53. We walk in abundance and we have dominion over earth's economic system
54. We are DEBT FREE and are not slaves to anyone
55. Wealth is transferred into OUR hands, NOW, BELIEVE IT AND RECEIVE IT
56. OUR income will always be greater than OUR expenses
57. Christ already paid the PRICE and by HIS STRIPES WE ARE HEALED
58. WE HAVE AN ABUNDANCE OF money that WE need for day-to-day expenses
59. WE always have more than enough to give
60. WE will sow great seeds and we will reap even better seeds
61. WE joyfully give a tenth of all our earnings to God
62. There is no lack in our house, business or relationships
63. We finance God's people. The homeless, widow, orphans and the less fortunate are taken care of by us
64. OUR bank accounts are filled

65. OUR network and net worth increase daily
66. We have a great network and net worth

I decree and declare that:

67. WE are resourceful
68. Everything THAT WE need is available to US when needed
69. The DOORS ARE WIDE OPEN, and no man can close it
70. WE will only speak and share the GOOD NEWS
71. WE will praise God in and out of season
72. OUR NEXT 7 YEARS ARE FILLED WITH ABUNDANCE
73. WE are transformed daily by renewing our minds
74. WE walk in the Supernatural and God's presence is always with us
75. Our SOUL is well
76. WE are loved and will show LOVE
77. This year is a good year
78. I decree and declare that you have stepped into your #**MEGA** Life and the #**MEGA** Cycle.
79. I decree that this is a good and prosperous year.

NOTES..........

Personal Prayer

(Pray Out Loud)

Our Father which art in Heaven, Hallowed, Mighty, Great and Powerful is your Name. Let your Kingdom come and let your will be done in my life. Thank you for my daily bread… (the word). Forgive me for all my sins and debts as I forgive those that have sinned against me. Help me when I am tempted and save me from the evil one. For thine is the Kingdom the Power and the Glory, forever in Jesus Name!

Complete your personal prayer that's specific to you.

Dear God:

_____

_____

_____

_____

Conclusion

"When he had received the drink, Jesus said, "It is finished. With that, he bowed his head and gave up his spirit."
John 19:30 NIV

Three (3) of the most powerful words that seals the deal in any area of life, are **"It is FINISHED."** When Jesus spoke that out of His mouth, He meant it. You are already pre-destined to finish what God placed in you. You were destined for greatness before the foundations of the world. It's not by coincidence why you are reading this book, it's by divine appointment.

It is time for you to truly walk out your **PURPOSE** and to live a life with meaning. You are alive for such a time as THIS! You can no longer run from the true authentic you. Proverbs

19:21 AMP reminds us that *"Many plans are in a man's mind, but it is the Lord's purpose for him that will stand"* and Romans 8:28 AMP *"We are assured and know that God being a partner in their labor all things work together and are fitting into a plan for good to and for those who love God and are called according to His design and purpose."* You are called according to HIS **PURPOSE**, so declare it and walk in it! YOUR TIME IS NOW!

Perhaps you have had some terrible years or maybe some great years. Perhaps you are going through a rough time right now, because there are still some fragments of the Reset that God is still ironing out. Perhaps you are fired up and ready to be the best you and to live the **MEGALiFE**, but you're a little scared. Maybe you've had several ups and downs and have felt like giving up. No matter what state of life you are in, this is the Year of New Beginnings where

God is making all things new again. You have the opportunity to start all over again. God is patient, faithful, thoughtful, kind, loving, and should I say **patient** again and His will and thoughts towards you are good.

God does not desire to see any of His people perish and it's His will that you should succeed. This is the year to see with the mind and not with the physical eyes. It's the year of 2nd Chances and a Fresh Start. God is saying that this year **5779/2019** is the year of new beginnings, the year of abundance, the year of life, the year of purpose and the **MEGA** Year, where He is personally **Making Everyday Good Again** and **Making Everything Good Again**. God saw that it was good when He created you, thus, you are His **good** creation.

NOTES..........

Whew! Pause! Take a moment and process all this MEGA Message. It's your moment to put your thoughts on paper. Journal the Journey.

Appreciation

First, I thank God for giving me life, health and strength and the many gifts to be who I am today. I thank Him for His son Jesus Christ, my savior and to the Holy Spirit for being my guide. Thanks to my husband Kevel A. Anderson, Sr., who loves me with all his heart and gives me the space and time that I need to live out my purpose in life. To our beautiful daughters, Christina and Chassidy and our son A.J. and nephew (like a son), C.J. for their love, laughter and support. To my mom, Sharon and a host of family and friends, thank you! Thanks to the publishing team and the staff at Riley Press (www.RileyPress.com), and anyone who had anything to do with this book being released. Most of all thank you for investing your time and resources. Thank you for being a part of my life!

About the Author

DR. CAROLYN G. ANDERSON is the FRESH, dynamic and inspirational VOICE that's creating a buzz locally, nationally and internationally. She's a Talk Show Host, TV & Radio Personality, Keynote Speaker, Wealth Coach, Professor and the author of several books such as Living a Wealthy LiFE on Purpose, The 10 Laws of Lead-er-SHIP, Heal-thy LiFE-Heal-thy Land, Focus & Get Results, Pregnant with a Promise, From the PIT to the PALACE and many more.

One of the nation's leading expert on the art of transformation, she is the Founder and Executive Vice President of Integrity Consulting and Coaching Enterprise (ICE), a corporate coaching, speaking and consulting firm with over 30 years of combined experience in strategic leadership, lean processes, six sigma, visioning, process improvement, coaching, contracting and negotiations, amongst other services.

A trained Army Soldier, Dr. Carolyn knows the discipline and FOCUS needed to hit the TARGET! She utilizes the same skills taught in the military to fight and WIN. She is a trusted voice and a ground-breaking Speaker-preneur. Amongst her many accomplishments and accolades, her all-time favorite role is being a mom and wife. Being a parent is a gift from God. She is purpose driven and lives life fully every day always walking in her divine calling. She's an ordained Prophet and a Senior Leader of:

Kingdom Church in U (CiU), a global ministry (www.ciuglobal.com). Learn more about her at www.carolynganderson.com or text DrCarolyn to 22828 to connect with her.

Be sure to share these hashtag **#megalife #mega #megalifemovement** as you are reading this book and as you begin to decree and declare what your seven (7) years of abundance will look like.

Join the MEGALiFE Movement on Facebook Groups
https://www.facebook.com/groups/
megalifemovement/ and let's stay connected.

Connect with us!

I would like to hear from you and your wonderful testimony from this book. You can email us at admin@carolynganderson.com or to join our Mailing List text DrCarolyn to 22828

Learn more about other products and services or for booking at **www.carolynganderson.com**

Like our Page
www.facebook.com/IamDrCarolyn1

Follow us at: www.twitter.com/IamDrCarolyn

Other Books by Dr. Carolyn

Pregnant with a Promise

Focus & Get Results

Heal-thy LiFE

Heal-thy Land

The MVP Year 2017   2018 MEGA Year

Heal-thy LiFE/Heal-thy Land 2nd Edition

The 10 Laws of Lead-er-SHIP

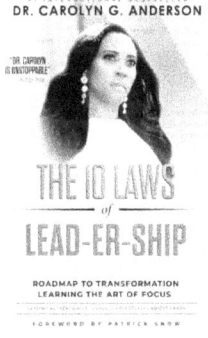

The MEGALiFE Matrix (8x10) Spiral

The MEGALiFE Matrix (8 ½ x 11) Bound

Write The Vision Lined Journal

Certified Coaching Manual

New in 2019

Living a Wealthy LiFE on Purpose

7 Steps to Break-through (Digital/Audio

What Happens When The Dream Dies?

#MEGALIFE Series

5780 - 2020 - Book 4
5781 - 2021 - Book 5
5782 - 2022 - Book 6
5783 - 2023 - Book 7

All Dr. Carolyn's books can be purchased here:
Https://www.amazon.com/author/carolynganderson

www.ingramcontent.com/pod-product-compliance
Lightning Source LLC
Chambersburg PA
CBHW071200160426
43196CB00011B/2146